Boss Beauty

Boss Beauty

INSPIRATION TO BE EVERYTHING YOU WANT

LISA MAYER

THE collective BOOK STUDIO

A woman can be everything she wants. Boss Beauties is a force to make it real.

Definition of a Boss Beauty

Boss Beauty *noun*

A woman who is in fearless pursuit of her dreams; one who is kind, confident, bold, brave, has grit and NEVER gives up. She is pursuing her many passions and knows her worth.

queens

owning t

in their

unapologeti

ridiculously

bringing out e

full stop

heir story

wn lane

cally femme

empowered

veryone's best

Design Your Life

Once upon a time I dreamed big. I wanted to empower young women.

My Story

I didn't grow up having business connections in the world. I grew up on a farm. While I'm so grateful for what I did have, it didn't include access to every single thing I needed to make my dream come true. That's a big part of my story, and why I have been inspired to help others. My mom, my stepmom, and my grandmothers were all super strong, so I had inspirational women around me. But I didn't have a career mentor until after college when I was in the work world.

A world where women can be everything they want has never existed. We believe Boss Beauties can be a force and provide a solution—and make this new world real. Women can be gamers, astronauts, caregivers, actors, physicians, race car drivers, CEOs—anything. A woman can be everything she wants.

I have been able to design the life and career I want, and I want to inspire you to do the same—to help you be confident, go for your dreams, and dream big. I want to give you opportunities to meet amazing incredible mentors and role models from all different industries, to read their words, and realize You Can Do It, too. To have an opportunity to get in deep and listen to these women be open about their struggles, challenges, the times they wanted to give up on their dreams but kept going.

When I started my first company (providing mentorship to women and girls worldwide), I built it from scratch. I did not have a lot of money. I did not have institutional venture funding or business partners with a lot of connections. I bootstrapped it as much as I could. In doing so, I realized that the part I have always wanted to share with young women is to Not Give Up—to help you know and hear that you can do this, regardless of the resources you have. Maybe you don't have a list of connections or a network with lots of CEOs and other influential people right now. Start by identifying what resources you do have and don't give up on your dreams. Beat down the door and say "let's work together"—even if it takes a lot of tries.

In the beginning, it was just me with my little company. It was intimidating.

I wasn't at a big company that gave me the credibility to get inside the building. I got a lot of No's; I had a lot of failures. But I kept getting up every single day and kept going in the face of setbacks. And then I found myself in corporate boardrooms with teams of senior executives to pitch a partnership. And they said YES. They wanted to partner with us, and we continued to build these connections, whether at Verizon or Apple or Barbie.

At Apple stores, we would host events for college students and bring in role models and mentors to speak with them. During the pandemic, I pulled together a virtual mentorship program that was a hybrid of a mentorship and an internship. On Zoom we'd bring in industry leaders to share insights and advice. But we'd also assign a few projects so young women could add skills to their resume—so when they were ready to go after their next internship, they had picked up experience during the remote program. Lots of students called me months later to relay this had helped them get an internship at Facebook or Google or Chanel—wherever they had dreamed of working. A lot has changed since I was growing up. There are so many resources for college students. You can join programs where you are a campus ambassador—and share that company with your campus while being mentored and learning from a professional.

The Story of Boss Beauties

My passion has always been about providing mentorship and giving access to the next generation of women to meet role models and find a way into the building. Sometimes part of it is just walking into the offices of *Vogue*. Or onto the floor of the New York Stock Exchange and getting to watch the opening bell. Even just passing through the doors of an office like that can help you feel more empowered and confident. Even just attending fashion week you might feel "I'm a part of this, I deserve to be here." I want to help you have these experiences. I want to remind you of your self-worth at every step of the way. When you gain access to these offices and board rooms, to a seat at the table, you meet and hear

and witness role models and gain a little extra confidence. I want to give you the ability to see and think "If she can do it, I can do it, too." Because you can.

When I was seven months pregnant, thinking about the future and where my career might go as a new mom, I found the Web3 space. I started exploring the Web3 world and found a very entrepreneurial community. So, I decided to launch Boss Beauties with a collection of digital collectibles featuring strong, confident, independent women with a portion of the proceeds going to make an impact. We immersed ourselves in the industry and learned as much as we could about it. Eight weeks later we launched the Boss Beauties collection in the fall of 2021. We sold out our collection of 10,000 digital collectibles in 90 minutes generating 2.3 million dollars. I was crying hysterically. I was holding my newborn Hudson in my lap and could not believe we'd raised the money to start a new company in that amount of time. That's how Boss Beauties was born—but it's the purpose behind it that is most important to me. We just so happen to have been born in the Web3 space. But what we're doing is not only about Web3 to me at all—it's the means to do the work that we're passionate about. Starting Boss Beauties was hard—I had a newborn and was running on no sleep—but giving up on my dream was not an option.

and a chef's coat. We wanted it to be clear that a woman can be everything that she wants, and you don't have to be described by just one thing. The caregiver illustration is special to me—we are all caregivers in some way. So is the CEO, president, queen, superhero, race car driver. You don't have to choose. You can be all of them.

Every day is International Women's Day to me. It's something that's important to us every day. Dream big, go for it.

Created by our designer Marion Ben-Lisa, each Boss Beauty has a unique array of personal attributes: facial features, hair, clothing, adornment, background. We wanted every Boss Beauty to be fierce, fearless, and confident. The colors are vibrant and bright, and feel strong. When you typically look at a portrait, you might see she is all one thing. Maybe she's an astronaut or a scientist, wearing a helmet or a suit, or she's an athlete or lawyer or teacher. We mixed up all the traits so she might be wearing an astronaut's helmet

In these pages, we've collected quotes and stories and artwork to inspire you to work toward your personal dreams. Words are so powerful. Your value is not just how many followers you have on social media or how much is in your bank account. I want you to know: *You* are valuable. You have value. You can be everything you want. Dream Big.

XO,
Lisa

> On the journey of life, your road is going to have some curves, forks, and roadblocks. Each of these challenges and choices present opportunities to create your personal journey. So take the time to enjoy the ride and make the time to look in the rearview mirror and absorb all you have learned. Own your own journey!
>
> —Yael Afriat

> You have to believe in your own light, even when it seems like no one else around you does. You deserve to be in spaces where your light can shine and surrounded by people who celebrate your brightness. Don't dim your light for anyone. Don't let your light be dimmed by anything. Even if no one else around you thinks you can do it, keep shining brightly and show them you can.
>
> —Lila Thomas

Harness the power of your intentions and desires by refusing to allow any obstacles to consume your mind. You will get challenged, but stay aware in the present moment and give yourself grace if something doesn't go your way. Don't see yourself through the eyes of the world—put your best efforts in and let the universe work its magic. Anything is possible and everything is achievable.

—Beenish Saeed

Lift as you climb.

—Eunice Olugbile

I AM

Confident
Powerful
Unstoppable
Successful
Grateful
Motivated
Enough
Creative
Inspiring

When You Don't Remember Your Self-Worth
Love Notes from Your Future Self

I AM

a mom. I am an entrepreneur. I am a CEO. I am a sister, a friend, and I am my own Boss Beauty Role Model. At a recent mentorship event, I asked a 9-year-old girl to tell me who her most inspiring role model was. Before she responded, I had predictions of whom she might say. I was waiting to hear which famous Olympian, scientist, astronaut, actress, politician, philanthropist, or well-known author she might choose as her favorite. She came back and said, "I am my most inspiring Role Model." Wow. This 9-year-old girl really spoke to me. Of course, we all have role models that motivate us to dream big and work hard. We all also need to remember that we are our best cheerleaders, our very best advocates. I love that statement: I am my own most inspiring Role Model. Give yourself some credit and remember that YOU, BB, are a BOSS.

I want to help you realize
'I'm a part of this. I deserve to be here.
If she can do it, I can do it, too.'

"Being unstoppable doesn't mean you don't have challenges along the way. It doesn't mean you never fall down or fail from time to time. Being unstoppable means getting back up every single time until you achieve your goal.

Barbara Corcoran once said: 'My best successes came off the heels of failure.' To be unstoppable, you don't have to not fail—you simply have to keep getting up and trying again each and every day. Did you know that Oprah was fired from one of her first jobs in TV? Oprah isn't unstoppable because she never experienced rejection. She's unstoppable because she fearlessly pursued her dreams. And didn't stop."

—Lisa Mayer

" I define swagger as showing up for yourself, defining your finish line, and having enough grit/grace/ hustle to get there.

—Robin Arzón

"

" Self-love and compassion allow us to show up for ourselves and others. That, for me, is where our individual power lies, which leads to purpose in all of life's moments. "

—Shira Lazar

"Take a moment to meditate and count your blessings. Whether it's your health, the health of your loved ones, or if you have a roof over your head. There are so many things that we can be thankful for. Look at that to make you stronger and fight for your next goal or dream. You have to come from a place of strength."

—Ming-Na Wen

"Whether it is through the best of times, or the not so easy times— take heart, reflect, and then identify, prioritize, and explore your passions. The world needs your light."

—Valerie Arioto

"The longest relationship we're ever going to have is with ourselves, so take care of yourself. Practice self-care, self-improvement, and self-discipline. Set goals, pay attention to your needs, ask for what you want, and enjoy the little things just for you. When in doubt, GO FOR IT, and make yourself proud.

—Julia Landauer

Pull your own chair up to the table. Scribble your own name on the VIP List, and don't let anyone tell you that you don't belong.

—Arlan Hamilton

"In a world that never stops, pause and savor the magic now. Each day brings precious moments worth cherishing. Be fully engaged, notice the beauty around you, and relish the simplest pleasures. Let go of worries and regrets. Today is a gift, an opportunity for happiness. Live it with intention, gratitude, and an open heart. Embrace the present, find joy in every moment."

—Maria Bravo

GRATEFUL

Creativity has always been core to who I am, and I was truly blessed to be able to build my career around it. Being creative has brought so much joy to my life and to so many others. It's a fundamental skill that can be applied to any career or passion.

—Ann Lewnes

"The minute you see someone who looks like you, who moves the way you move, it gives hope to younger generations to show them that anything is possible. You can do what you want.

—Lesego Mogonediwa

Say yes now, then figure out how.

—Jaime Schmidt

"Like so many people, I struggle with imposter syndrome. All. The. Time. When it creeps up on me, I try to remind myself of two things. First, someone else is watching and observing how I behave in that moment. I allow myself to be vulnerable, sometimes even saying out loud I am nervous or don't feel like I belong in that space—to validate that it's ok if anyone else is feeling this way. Second, to remind myself that if I am in that room, it's because I was invited to do so. Someone believed in me and opened a door. If you were asked to be there, it's because you deserve to be there. Someone opened the door and all you need to do is be confident enough to walk through it—so do it."

—Heather Hatlo Porter

"It's your inner truth. If you're doing your best work and you think it's work that helps other people, who can tear you down?

—Brit Morin"

Remembering My Self-Worth

Early on in my entrepreneurial journey there was a time when I had just $7 left in the bank. Although I almost gave up, I knew it wasn't time to quit. At that moment, I took a screenshot of my bank balance and decided to keep building. There are always going to be challenges in life or business. Whether you have your own $7 moment, or another type of challenge that makes you want to quit, I urge you to keep going! There is nothing that cannot be figured out or solved. Whether you have $7 or $7 million in the bank, your bank account doesn't dictate your value. Keep going, keep building, and remember your worth.

When You Don't Remember Your Self-Worth

A queen walks amongst us.

Life can be tough, life can be rough, but do remember you're more than enough.

With her head in the star-filled night sky—not in the clouds—she signifies the dreams everyone has.

You're never an overnight success. It might look that way on Instagram or in the press, but there are so many hard lessons. KEEP GOING.

Love Note from My Future Self

Lisa,

Your future self is cheering you on. The five-year-old Lisa who grew up on a farm and was shy and insecure in school would have never thought she'd have the courage to start a business, partner with the #1 fashion doll in the world, or build a community with a reach of one billion in its first year. That little girl was not confident. Look at where she is now! Your FUTURE self is cheering you on at every stage. Remember—the more you build, the more Boss Beauties we can impact. Remember that some of your best successes have come right after your biggest failures. Let's Go Boss Beauty. Go BB, Go!

XO,
Lisa

Love Notes from Your Future Self

Find your passion. Climb that mountain.
Then take a good look around at your surroundings.
What are the nearby peaks that you can explore?
How can you expand your scope and
bring your unique spark somewhere new?
Both fuel and protect your passion.

Success is right
around the corner.
You got this BB!

Celebrate every
mile and make
sure you get
a photo taken
with your well-
deserved medal.

From one Boss Beauty to
another, enjoy your ride
because this, my dear, is your
life unfolding. It's incredible
as well as incredibly messy.
You are your own boss, so
walk right through the door
that you choose.

EMPOWERING

Success
Happiness
Self-Love
Clarity
Abundance
Change
Confidence
Courage
Healing
Motivation

Before that Big Moment
Monday Motivation

Empowering Dreams

The power of visualizing my dreams has always had a major impact on my life and career. Back in 2015, I attended a summit hosted by the United States of Women at the White House. When I looked up the list of speakers, I saw the name of a woman who was the White House Chief Technology Officer. I was working on a partnership with Verizon and Apple at the time, and we were about to host an event featuring inspirational women in tech. I really wanted that specific speaker to be involved in some way.

The next morning before attending the summit, I did something I normally would not have. I decided to get my hair done thinking it would help me feel confident and ready to take on the day. I went into a local Drybar and sat down in a seat. As I looked to my right, I realized the woman to my left was the very woman I was hoping to meet! We had a 45-minute conversation, and that evening I found myself at her dinner party, meeting over 50 of the most inspiring and powerful women in tech. Later at the summit, I sat down to listen to a fireside chat hosted by Michelle Obama and Oprah and remember thinking how inspiring it would be to meet them both one day. A year later, I found myself on *The Tonight Show with Jimmy Fallon* recording a video for Michelle Obama. Little did I know, she was hiding behind a curtain ready to surprise me. She walked out and we got to share a few words about our shared passion for educating women and girls.

I'm still waiting for that moment with Oprah, and I'm certainly not saying everything I've manifested or dreamed about has happened. However, I do believe that your thoughts and dreams have an impact on how you show up each and every day as you work towards your goals in business or life. Keep manifesting the dreams in your heart—even the ones that might seem impossible. I'm cheering you on, BB!

I'm not my disability.
My disability is my
story. You can't control
how you are born,
but you can control
how you live.

—Clara Woods

Break records. Break barriers. I'll fight so she doesn't have to.

—Allyson Felix

"Learn to advocate for yourself the way you would for a best friend. If you wouldn't tolerate those same things that you're saying to yourself being said to someone you love and respect, then surely you have to interrupt that voice. Back yourself.

—Jameela Jamil

"Throughout my career, change has consistently shaped my journey, presenting unexpected opportunities for growth and learning. It has been a powerful teacher, propelling me to adapt and overcome challenges along the way. The road hasn't always been smooth, and I've encountered my fair share of bumps, failures, and humbling experiences. However, each one has proven to be a valuable chance to gain wisdom and develop resilience.

—Esther Lem

Stop hoping for a promotion that's not coming. Instead, start a business at which you want to work.

—Sallie Krawcheck

"I like to say 'When purpose meets passion, you're unstoppable.' Pay attention to what sets your soul on fire and go after it boldly and bravely. Trying isn't part of my vocabulary. I believe you're either going to do something, or you're not. Embrace failure as part of the process but know that there's always a solution—you just have to find it.

—Shelley Zalis

"Remember to hold on to your power and intuitive self-wisdom. There are many times when you are blazing a trail, uncovering new ways of being in the world, which can challenge the way others may think and your center becomes unbalanced. The moment when you decide not to give up is when you find your power."

—Sasha Wallinger

"Learning to continually trust and use your voice and silence the voices of others in your mind is a challenge I continue to face. It requires a lot of confidence in what you're doing. And that takes practice."

—Kim DeJesús

Life is full of colossal challenges. Main key to success: How do you eat an elephant? One bite at a time.

—Martha Delehanty

Believe what you know about yourself and not what you're told about yourself.

—Danette Anderson

"

Use your voice—even when it shakes.

—Robin Arzón

"

"Don't settle for anything in life. Go after what you want and what you're passionate about. If there isn't 'such a thing' then make it a thing. Be authentically you at all times.

—Kelsey Stewart

She's beautiful and don't let anyone tell her different.

—Dr. Chisom Ikeji

On Staying Calm and Confident

So many of us get nervous going into a big meeting, pitching an idea, or speaking publicly. Even the world's most successful CEOs, who run billion-dollar companies, have those moments. What matters is that you show up. Go in with your head held high. Remember, confidence is always on trend. Wear confidence and wear it well. Confidence is your all-purpose wardrobe for every big moment.

Before that Big Moment

Design your next adventure.
It may come with the thrill of spontaneity, the nervousness of the unknown, or the excitement of new beginnings. Fulfilling new experiences are some of the things that make having new adventures worthwhile. The anticipation of what's next is what keeps us going.

I am here to tell you that
YOU CAN DO IT,
YOU ARE GOOD ENOUGH,
YOU ADD VALUE. If you can remember this, you will become unstoppable.
You control your destiny.

Know your worth.
They'd be lucky to partner with you.
You're offering them an opportunity
to work with you.

There is a time and place for everyone. Seize your opportunities and bust through those doors.

Reframing Mondays

I recently spoke to my friend and fellow Boss Beauty, Pili, who shared with me what she calls her "Love Letter to Monday." In this letter she wrote:

"Can we be nicer to Mondays? Mondays can be a chance at something better. Mondays can be a time to get it right. Mondays can be a great day to have a great day. So, Monday, I choose to see the good in you. I choose to deal with, correct, work out, and find solutions for all the items you put on my Monday plate."

I imagine most people have a similar feeling when they think of Monday. Whether you're starting a business, training for a marathon, studying for a big test, or simply trying to find the motivation to take the very first step towards a big dream you have, it might be hard to find motivation on Monday. You might feel overwhelmed by all that you need to climb the entire staircase, but let's start with one small step. What is it that you need to do today, on Monday? What do you need to do to simply climb up one more step? Go do that. Small steps, taken daily, lead to big results.

Monday Motivation

You get to create memories and moments that define who you are and become snapshots of your life. This journey is uniquely yours. Define it, embrace it, revel in it. What will you be tasting next?

Be your own love of your life. Don't chase others to find your ride or die.

Take it one day at a time, BB. There are so many moments when the goal seems impossible and you don't quite know how to get started. Take it one step at a time, and soon you'll see you've climbed the entire staircase.

Be a woman who speaks her truth. Be a woman who is bold and brave. Be a woman who possesses grit. Be a woman who expresses what's on her mind. Be a woman who overcomes self-doubt. Be a woman who breaks boundaries. Be a woman who stands up for herself. Be a woman who empowers others. Be a women who doesn't quit in the face of obstacles. Be a Boss Beauty.

ACT WITH

Kindness

Encouragement

Grace

Compassion

Thoughtfulness

Honesty

Passion

Advice from Your Big Sis
When You Feel Like Giving Up

ACT WITH

authenticity. Be yourself. There are so many times when we're told to be less this, or more that. Acting with authenticity means staying true to exactly who you are and being unapologetically the Boss Beauty you were meant to be. If it doesn't feel like YOU, don't force it.

There are times when I know I have to speak from my heart. But, it can be hard to find the right words. We're afraid of making the wrong statement or impression. It's okay to be nervous. None of us are perfect. Sharing your authentic self is vital.

When you're feeling doubtful and wonder if your dream, goal, or purpose in life will ever be fulfilled–stop, take a moment, and believe what's for you will never ever miss you.

—Jully Black

As a CEO and a woman in business, I can't tell you how many times I've been told to be less kind. Being kind doesn't mean being weak. You can be equally kind, confident, and assertive. You can get ahead in business and be bold without sacrificing your own values.

One of my role models, Fran Hauser, who was the former President of Time Inc., featured me in her bestselling book *Myth of the Nice Girl*. In her book, Fran wrote something that really impacted me. Fran said kindness is a superpower. I couldn't agree more.

—Lisa Mayer

"One of the greatest gifts we can extend to ourselves is the space and grace to change, evolve, come together to fall apart, and take our time as we ride those ever-changing waves. So be patient and lean into the freedom and the fun of living your own pace. With patience, you unlock a layer of self-love and presence that pours into everything you do. Giving yourself time is like an affirmation, reminding you that you are enough, always right on time, wherever you are in life."

—Haile Thomas

Make your younger self proud. Pursue your goals with so much passion and persistence that the younger version of you would be shocked at what you've achieved. I recently read this quote from one of my mentors and investors, Adrianna Samaniego: 'It was also for the younger version of myself, who needed to see myself in these rooms and know it was possible.' I love this sentiment. Do it for your younger self. Show yourself what is possible.

—Lisa Mayer

"If you are feeling isolated or alone, look outside the company you are in. There are probably other women in your industry that are feeling the same way, or an adjacent industry and forming that peer mentor group will really help boost you up and lift everyone up together.

—Randi Zuckerberg

"Leadership is not about you. It's about the people you are trying to lead. It's a special relationship in which the best leaders help others experience a higher version of themselves. It's a choice–not a title–and a choice that you can make every day of your career. So, ask yourself how you can help others be THEIR best selves. Lift as you climb, and you will be a leader that others want to follow. You will knit together a quilt of relationships that will catch you when you fall and propel you forward when you need a rocket booster.

—Judith Spitz

Give yourself permission to stop asking for permission.

—Rebecca Minkoff

"I was talking badly about myself to my best friend. And she said 'Why are you talking that way about my best friend? I think she is amazing and all these things.' She defended me to myself. You have to be your own best friend."

—Lisa Mayer

"I've always had my eye on 'what's next, how am I going to be challenged?'—that's what really motivates me. I love a challenge. I love to fix things. Give me something that needs polishing or fixing or reimagining."

—Stephanie Dobbs Brown

Nice is your Superpower.

—Fran Hauser

"There are battles to be fought on so many different fronts. But, we just have to start, put one foot in front of the other and keep going. We have to be driven by hope. We just have to start.

—Tara Abrahams

"You have to believe in yourself and the vision and not be afraid of rejection—that's part of the journey. Tied to that obviously is resilience. Waking up every day and finding the energy and the strength to keep going and deal with the setbacks that come with starting something from scratch.

—Anu Duggal

Being a boss doesn't mean being hard and tough, though you will have to fight for people and causes you believe in.
It means loving freely and fiercely, serving fiercely, leading patiently, learning and knowing when to say yes (to only the right things for you or the collective good).
Remember: A righteous No is more powerful than a lukewarm Yes. If you seek only praise, likes, or popular opinion, you will never have peace; every person has their own unique God-given beauty and mission that only you can fulfill and protect. Trust that and pursue it!

—Xian Horn

"I'm not afraid to fail at all. Certainly not afraid to take any risks, and I think that's what allowed me to move to so many different cities. To me, if it didn't work out I'd just move somewhere else. It's not the end of the world. I think that's what afforded me a lot of space and flexibility that allowed me to take some chances that I wouldn't have otherwise."

—Stephanie Dobbs Brown

Advice from a Friend Who Has Helped Me

Back in 2016, Rebecca Minkoff invited some of our Gen Z community behind the scenes to experience a mentorship opportunity at New York Fashion Week. These Gen Z women had the opportunity to interview Rebecca with *Teen Vogue* magazine! After that day, I remember hearing this quote from Rebecca and it has inspired me ever since:

> "In every life phase, you'll be confronted with something that scares you. And you have to go into it being as fearless as you can."

If you're dreaming big, there will always be something scary. Be as fearless as you can. Remember that even the most powerful CEOs, actresses, and pro-athletes get nervous at times. It doesn't mean they aren't scared or nervous, but they simply walk into that board room, onto that film set, or out to the field to compete and perform. They brush off the fear and give it their best. That's what makes them successful.

Advice from Your Big Sis

Your looks and clothing will change with time, but your pride? That is something you must never leave home without.

Speak with kindness and confidence.

Learn to fall in love with yourself exactly as you are, BB.

How can you expand your scope and bring your unique spark somewhere new? Both fuel and protect your passion.

On Not Giving Up

Have you ever had a moment where you ALMOST gave up on a dream only later to find out that you were actually just one conversation, one rehearsal, one practice, or one meeting away from achieving that big goal that you never thought might be possible? Every time you feel like you can't take another step, remember that moment. How would your future self have felt if you had given up the moment right before you succeeded? Your future self will be so proud of you for taking one more step forward. You got this Boss Beauty!

When you hear the word *no*, keep in mind that it doesn't necessarily mean no. It could just mean not yet. It doesn't mean never. Don't take *no* for an answer. Be persistent. Maybe the timing isn't right for that partnership or collaboration, but it could mean it's not going to happen yet. Don't be afraid to ask again.

When You Feel Like Giving Up

I challenge you to make a list of 30 things that make you YOU! Keep this list on hand. Whenever you're feeling down or overwhelmed, you have it to reference. You are unique, you are one of a kind!

Perseverance, dedication, and a little spunk is all you really need.

The moment you feel like quitting could be the moment just before you succeed.

Glance behind you and create speed and momentum for the ones who will build off your legacy.

Take the Boss Beauty Challenge

I Am...

I Am Manifesting...

_____

_____

_____

_____

_____

_____

_____

_____

I Act with...

Contributors

Tara Abrahams currently serves as Head of Impact at The Meteor, a new media company that amplifies the voices of women—through storytelling, journalism, and art. Tara is also the founder of *Kahani*, a new print magazine by girls and for girls globally. Tara also serves as board chair of She's the First, an organization that fights for a world in which every girl chooses her own future. Prior to her role at The Meteor, Tara served as managing director at Arabella Advisors, led the start-up phase at VOW to end child marriage, and was the executive director of the Girl Project at *Glamour*.

Yael Afriat is the Chief Commercial and Revenue Officer for Boss Beauties. She has dedicated her career to bringing kids' entertainment, celebrity, fashion, and media brands to life via innovative products, programs, and partnerships. She is a founding member of Chief and 32Cents as well as a mother, wife, friend, yoga enthusiast, and traveler.

Danette Anderson is a professional photographer who found her niche when she started working with women. She has been both in front of and behind the lens, so she knows how to photograph women in a way that makes them look incredible, while also making them feel confident. Over the years, she has worked with hundreds of female clients, including high-profile celebrities and owners of national brands.

Valerie Arioto was a collegiate All-American and 2012 Pac-12 Player of the Year, medal-winning Olympian, and softball first baseman. She was a pitcher and infielder for the Cal Berkeley Golden Bears. She also was a member of the United States Women's National Team for 11 seasons from 2011–2021, and at the 2020 Tokyo Summer Olympics helped Team USA win a silver medal.

Robin Arzón is the founder of Swagger Society and serves as VP and Head Instructor at Peloton. She excels at everything she sets out to do—twenty-seven-time marathoner, two-time *New York Times* bestselling author, *Glamour* magazine's inaugural "Daring to Disrupt" award winner, named to *Fortune* magazine's 40 Under 40 in 2020, and MasterClass instructor on mental strength. Robin has become a leader in Web3 by founding its first lifestyle membership club.

Jully Black has been called a visionary, a trailblazer, a truth-teller, and a Canadian icon. This multiple JUNO Award–winning singer and one of Canada's Walk of Fame inductees is a platinum-selling recording artist, named one of the 25 Greatest Canadian Singers Ever. She is also an extremely talented actress, entrepreneur, motivational speaker, and fitness leader whose philanthropic work has taken her to villages from Bangladesh to South Africa, across Canada and the United States. She has written songs for and collaborated with industry heavyweights including Nas, Destiny's Child, and Ian Thornley (Big Wreck). As a performer, she's torn up stages alongside such artists as Alicia Keys, Elton John, Celine Dion, and Jessie Reyez. Her wildly successful 360 health and wellness programs 100 Strong and Sexy, The Power of Step, and her charity the Jully Black Family Foundation are a part of her ongoing mission to "help people love themselves a little bit more each and every day."

Maria Bravo is a Spanish actress, entrepreneur, and philanthropist. She is also the founder of the Global Gift Foundation and Global Gift Platform, an international nonprofit foundation whose objective is to positively impact the lives of vulnerable children and empower women. Lastly, she is the founder and CEO of Maupy Worldwide, a boutique talent agency.

Stephanie Dobbs Brown is the Chief Marketing Officer at Intercontinental Exchange (ICE), a Fortune 500 data and technology company and the parent company of the New York Stock Exchange. In 2022, Stephanie led all aspects of ICE's rebrand, a cohesive repositioning that links the company's global expertise in designing, building, and operating digital marketplaces and networks that connect people to opportunity. As part of the rebrand, she launched ICE's commercial campaign and facilitated strategic partnerships with McLaren Racing and CNBC's *Mad Money*. She also forged a partnership with fashion house Balenciaga to debut its spring 2023 collection on the trading floor of the New York Stock Exchange, an unexpected move to reach new audiences and further cement its place at the heart of the cultural zeitgeist. Stephanie has spent her career building brands and global enterprises.

Kim DeJesús is an artist most notably known for her paintings that are influenced by her curiosity in how memory works and what it reveals about us and the world. She trained at Arizona State University, where she was the recipient of the Katherine K. Herberger Painting Scholarship, and received a postgraduate degree in art from North Central College in Naperville, Illinois.

Martha Delehanty serves as the Chief People Officer at Commvault, where she's responsible for all human resources strategies and programs. She has been a powerful advocate for young women in science, technology, engineering, and mathematics (STEM), helping drive participation in programs like Girls Who Code, Black Girls Code, Built By Girls, and Break Through Tech.

Anu Duggal is the founding partner of Female Founders Fund. Female Founders Fund has become the leading source of institutional capital for female founders, raising seed capital with over $3 billion in enterprise value. In 2018, Anu was included in *Fortune* magazine's 40 Under 40 list, and she has been praised for her impact in diversifying venture capital with additional distinctions, including *Business Insider*'s Ultimate List of Female Startup Investors and Top 4 Venture Firms Investing in Women.

Allyson Felix's advocacy has forever changed sports for women. She spoke out publicly about the inequality facing sponsored women athletes and called for industry-wide change. As a result, several major athletic sponsors have announced maternity protection and changed corporate policies, guaranteeing athletes' pay and bonuses through, and after, pregnancy. After her advocacy created a ripple effect of positive change in sports, she felt more energized than ever for her next adventure. So, Allyson teamed up with her brother, Wes, and together they built Saysh, a collection of stylish, functional sneakers designed for everyday performance.

Arlan Hamilton built a venture capital fund from the ground up, while homeless. She is the founder and managing partner of Backstage Capital. Backstage Capital is a venture capital seed fund investing exclusively in startups that are led by underrepresented founders. Starting from scratch in 2015,

Backstage has now raised more than $20 million and has invested in more than two hundred startup companies. Arlan is also the author of *It's About Damn Time* and *Your First Million: Why You Don't Have to Be Born into a Legacy of Wealth to Leave One Behind.*

Fran Hauser is a startup investor who is passionate about leveling the playing field for women. She has invested in more than 30 female-founded companies and is a pioneer in the movement to provide women more access to venture capital funding. As an advocate for women in business, she has written two award-winning books, *The Myth of the Nice Girl* and *Embrace the Work, Love Your Career.* She regularly speaks at conferences and organizations to help women build careers they love while staying true to themselves. Earlier in her career, she held executive leadership roles at Time Inc.'s *People, InStyle,* and *Entertainment Weekly* as well as at AOL and Coca-Cola.

Xian Horn is a joyful half-Asian woman with Cerebral Palsy and serves as founder of the nonprofit Give Beauty Wings. She is an advocate, speaker, blogger, and xxemplar for the AT&T NYU Connect Ability Challenge in the creation of assistive technology. Xian has been featured in the White House blog's Women Working to Do Good series, the *New York Times,* NPR, *Forbes, Fortune, Fast Company,* Bloomberg News, NBC News, Fox 5, and NY1 among others. Finally, in addition to Thrive Global, she is a blogger for Positively Positive, a community of more than 2.5 million readers, and ForbesWomen, writing on leadership, empowerment, and disability.

Chisom Ikeji is a board-certified physician in internal medicine, geriatrics and critical care medicine at the University of Pittsburgh Medical Center. Outside of work she enjoys creating health and skincare tip videos on social media.

Jameela Jamil is a one-of-a-kind multi-hyphenate who is an actress, writer, host, and activist. As an advocate for body positivity, she launched a movement and allyship platform called I Weigh—a platform and community of changemakers who come together to share ideas and experiences, and ultimately mobilize activism, exploring social issues that stem from mental health to climate change to the representation of marginalized groups. In April 2020, the I Weigh with Jameela Jamil podcast launched, in which Jameela speaks with a variety of thought-leaders, performers, activists, influencers, and friends about their own experiences and stories with their mental health. Jameela was first seen on American television starring as Tahani in Mike Schur's Golden Globe–nominated series *The Good Place.* Jameela was a judge on HBO Max's hit competition show, *Legendary,* as well as the host of the Impractical Jokers game show *The Misery Index.* Jameela has officially joined the Marvel Cinematic Universe in Disney+'s *She Hulk,* where she originated the first on-screen role of the Marvel villain Titania. She also starred on Peacock's comedy series *Pitch Perfect: Bumper in Berlin* in the role of Gisela. Jameela also lends her voice to the role of Wonder Woman in the DC Comics *DC League of Super-Pets* as well as the role of Ascenia on *Star Trek: Prodigy.* She hosts and executive produces Bad Dates, an original SmartLess Media podcast, where each week Jameela's favorite comedians, celebrities, and funny friends share their epic and true dating nightmares and misfires. The hilarious podcast debuted at #1 on the Apple Podcast Comedy Charts.

Sallie Krawcheck is the cofounder and CEO of Ellevest, an innovative digital investment platform designed to help women reach their financial goals. She is also chair of Ellevate Network, a professional networking community whose mission is to advance women in business. She is one of the highest ranked women ever to have worked on Wall Street, having held posts such as CEO of Smith Barney, CEO of Merrill Lynch Wealth Management, and CFO of Citigroup. She is one of the most-read "Influencers" on LinkedIn and has been profiled as one of *Fast Company*'s "Most Creative People" in business, as well as in the *Wall Street Journal*, *Fortune*, *Forbes*, and more.

Julia Landauer is a two-time champion racecar driver from New York City, having most recently raced in the NASCAR Xfinity Series. She's raced all over the world, including in the NASCAR Euro Series, where she finished fifth overall, the highest ever for an American. Away from the track, Julia graduated from Stanford University, earning a Bachelor of Science degree in Science, Technology, and Society. Her time in college inspired her to build her brand to be where technology, community, and racing intersect and fuse, while advocating for STEM education and women's empowerment. Julia is also a motivational keynote speaker, and she hosts the podcast If I'm Honest with Julia Landauer.

Shira Lazar is an Emmy-nominated host, producer, and content creator covering social media, AI, Web3, and digital wellness. She is also the CEO and cofounder of the publisher and digital media brand What's Trending.

Esther Lem As Chief Marketing Officer for Chegg, Esther oversees all aspects of the Chegg brand and the end-to-end user experience. Prior to joining Chegg, Esther held senior marketing roles at Unilever, across many global brands, including Dove and Axe. At Chegg, she has been instrumental in creating impactful marketing programs that resonate with the audience and build affinity as a leading student brand.

Ann Lewnes has a deep passion for creativity and storytelling, and supports the work of under-represented filmmakers and artists. She is on the boards of Mattel, the Sundance Institute, and Lehigh University.

Rebecca Minkoff, after developing an affinity for design while in the costume department in high school, moved to New York City at only eighteen years old to pursue her dream of becoming a fashion designer. In 2001, Rebecca designed a version of the "I Love New York" T-shirt as part of a five-piece capsule collection. In 2005, she designed her first handbag, which she soon dubbed the "Morning After Bag," a.k.a. the M.A.B. This iconic bag ignited Rebecca's career as a handbag designer and inspired her edgy, feminine creations in the years to come. Today, Rebecca Minkoff is a global brand with a wide range of apparel, handbags, footwear, jewelry, and accessories. In September 2018, she established the Female Founder Collective, a network of businesses led by women that invests in women's financial power across the socioeconomic spectrum by enabling and empowering female-owned businesses.

Lesego Mogonediwa is a pilot, mentor, and content creator. She uses her platforms to empower women by helping aspiring pilots navigate the aviation world through her videos on various social media platforms.

Brit Morin is a multifaceted individual, encompassing roles as a venture capitalist, serial entrepreneur, CEO, technologist, and dedicated creative. She cofounded and manages Offline Ventures, an early-stage venture studio focused on incubating companies at the convergence of online and offline realms. As an advocate for innovative tech and underrepresented founders, Brit invests in companies like Kindbody, Bobbie, and Cofertility. She's the driving force behind successful media and Web3 ventures like BFF, a pioneering community for educating and empowering women and nonbinary individuals in crypto and Web3, as well as the CEO of Brit + Co, a dynamic lifestyle and education enterprise catering to creatively inclined women. With numerous female learners, distributed products, and online class enrollments, Brit + Co stands as a premier platform for female learning and exploration. Brit's podcast, First in Line, connects and empowers listeners by unveiling emerging trends, while her book *Homemakers: A Domestic Handbook for the Digital Generation* and regular media appearances underscore her influence and reach.

Eunice Olugbile is the passionate social media manager behind Boss Beauties. She feels like her true self when she's exploring new destinations, trying new foods, and capturing her adventures. Her zest for life, constant curiosity, and commitment to empowering women and students make her a true Boss Beauty in both the digital and real worlds.

Heather Hatlo Porter serves as the Chief Communications Officer at Chegg, leading all internal and external global communications and philanthropic efforts for the company. While her career and work in brand storytelling and social impact is something she is very proud of, her most important roles include being a mom, a wife, and a big sister to six Boss Beauties.

Beenish Saeed is an award-winning speaker, author, and founder. Currently serving as the Director of Operations for Boss Beauties, she was named one of the 110 Most Inspirational Women of the Metaverse by Unstoppable Domains and Top 100 Women of the Future by Mission Impact Academy. She has worked with household entertainment, fashion, and luxury brands. She co-authored a book with the British Computer Society and is the founder of Like Minded Females Network Toronto and Halfeti, an exclusive private members' club for fashion executives in the UK and UAE.

Jaime Schmidt is an entrepreneur most known for founding Schmidt's Naturals, a brand she scaled from her kitchen to an acquisition by CPG giant, Unilever. She is also an investor and co-owner of Color Capital, a fund that invests in consumer products and emerging technologies. Jaime is the author of *Supermaker: Crafting Business on Your Own Terms*, a personalized guide on how to put your business on the map and turn your passion into profit. Most recently, she cofounded BFF, a company empowering others to explore the opportunities in Web3 through education and connection.

Judith Spitz is a technology and communications leader who served as the Chief Information Officer at Verizon. On a mission to create a world where women not only gain access to the technology field, but also become the next generation of technology leaders, Judy founded Break Through Tech, a national initiative launched at Cornell Tech. In 2021, she was honored to be on *Forbes* magazine's list of 50 Over 50 Women of Impact.

Kelsey Stewart is an American softball player and has been a member of the United States women's national softball team since 2014. She was a member of the national softball team that won an Olympic silver medal in the Summer 2020 Olympics.

Haile Thomas is a wellness and compassion activist, international speaker, author of *Living Lively: 80 Plant-Based Recipes to Activate Your Power and Feed Your Potential*, and CEO of the wellness teahouse Matcha Thomas. Through these avenues, her mission finds its wings—inviting people of all ages around the globe to explore and nurture their world within, unlocking our innate ability to make a mindful, meaningful, and heart-centered impact in our communities and beyond.

Lila Thomas has spent the last ten years working for brands doing good in the world. She leads all brand and impact initiatives at Boss Beauties, but what brings her the most joy is spending time with her family and two precious boys. Lila has always stayed busy—from playing competitive golf at Stanford to studying the harp and the piano from a young age through college, she aspires to show her boys they can truly be everything they want to be.

Sasha Wallinger is a Web3 & Foresight Strategist and Founder, who led has global brands as a Chief Marketing Officer. Her achievements curating pop-culture trends in fashion, sustainability, and wellness, translating to emerging technology audiences, inspired her to shape Blockchain Style Lab, in 2015, to harness the power of the creativity, collaboration, and community prevalent across Web3 to inform design and data across physical and digital ecosystems

Ming-Na Wen is an actress best known as the voice of the fearless and classic animated character Mulan. Her breakthrough role was in the *Joy Luck Club*, and she was honored as a Disney Legend in 2019. Ming-Na is also a Marvel hero, portraying agent Melinda May in *Marvel's Agents of S.H.I.E.L.D.* Most recently, Ming-Na played Fennec Shand in *The Mandalorian* and *The Book of Boba Fett* and Janet Stone in *Hacks*. She was also honored with a star on the Hollywood Walk of Fame in May 2023.

Clara Woods is a painter, artist, and model who experienced a prenatal stroke. As a result, she cannot read, write, or speak. However, she does understand Portuguese, Italian, and English. In 2018, with the support of her family, Clara was inspired by Frida Kahlo, her muse, to make her first exhibition. This exhibition took place in Florence, Italy, where Clara was born. Since then, Clara has made around thirty exhibitions on three continents, and in 2021, Louis Vuitton hosted Clara's art show in Art Basel Miami Beach. She has sold more than 700 paintings internationally and moved to California after receiving her American visa as an extraordinary talent.

Shelley Zalis Known as the "Chief Troublemaker," Shelley is a trailblazer for women in the workplace. She is an internationally renowned entrepreneur, a pioneer for online research, a sought-after speaker, a well-known thought leader, and a devoted mentor. As founder and CEO of The Female Quotient, Shelley is in the business of equality. Together with a growing global community of 1 million-plus conscious leaders, she is on a mission to change the equation and close the gender gap.

Randi Zuckerberg a former Silicon Valley professional, strongly advocates for the synergy between technology and the arts. Her decision to leave her successful career to pursue a role in Broadway's *Rock of Ages* proved fruitful as she earned three Tony awards. Now, she serves as an advisor, investor, and board member in the Web3 space, possessing rare expertise and credibility in groundbreaking technology and the creative arts. She sees the emerging Web3 leaders as fearless entrepreneurs who skillfully navigate the intersection of art and technology. Drawing from her experiences in the Web2 world and her success in leading artistic ventures, she eagerly looks forward to nurturing the next generation of billion-dollar brands that harmoniously integrate these two domains.

Acknowledgments

To my all-time favorite partner in business and life, Anthony, thank you for giving up your fifteen-plus-year career to build Boss Beauties. You're an Emmy Award–winning creative director, and you achieved so much long before Boss Beauties came into this world. You never had to leave that behind to build this company, but that shows just how much you care about our mission. You work tirelessly each and every day, often behind the scenes, with creativity, passion, and determination. I'm forever grateful that you made the decision to be my cofounder.

To my son, Hudson, thank you for bringing fun and adventure to my life each and every day! Being an entrepreneur and CEO is one of my favorite jobs, but being your mama is my most meaningful job title. Boss Beauties was born when you were a newborn, and you've played a special part of our story since you were just three months old. Being an entrepreneur takes so much grit and perseverance, and there's nothing better than spending time with you after a long day of work.

To Valentina, I love being your stepmom (aka bonus mom!). You make me proud. Keep dancing your way through life. Your passion, hard work, strength, and kindness will never lead you wrong. I'm always cheering you on!

To my parents, thank you for showing me the way. You each taught me something unique about life, integrity, and hard work. You sacrificed so much to give me opportunities that allowed me to pursue my dreams. You gave me a positive and nurturing environment and always encouraged me to try my best without putting pressure on me to strive for perfection. That environment is what enabled me to pursue work in entrepreneurship, knowing that failure and rejection are never the final answer. It's how many times you get back up after a challenge that allows you to keep going.

This book titled *Boss Beauty* could never go to market without mentioning my nieces, Abby, Genny, Nora, and Ella. I hope the wisdom and quotes in this book inspire you to dream big in everything you do.

To our Boss Beauties Dream Team members who have helped bring this book together, Elaine, Beenish, Yael, Kylie, Lila, and Eunice—each and every one of you have been part of making this book possible. We couldn't have done this without any of you. Your attention to detail, ability to manage deadlines, creativity, resourcefulness, and problem solving have all helped us make this come to fruition.

To Marion Ben-Lisa, our incredible artist, thank you for sharing your art with the world through Boss Beauties. As soon as I saw your art, I knew I had to collaborate with you to bring my vision for the brand to life.

To our Boss Beauties community, I am forever grateful to you! Whether I'm giving you a hug at an IRL event or chatting with you in our discord, I cherish every single moment. Your creativity and storytelling brought your BBs to life for me, and it meant so much to hear you creating such powerful stories about your BBs. It's an honor to share these stories in our first ever Boss Beauties book!

To our BB investors: Offline Ventures, Brit Morin, and James Higa, board member, Randi Zuckerberg, Female Founders Fund: Anu Duggal and Adrianna Samaniego, and Serena Ventures: Serena Williams, Allison Rappaport, Olivia Griffian, Pavan Sethi, Wieden+Kennedy, and Jaime Schmidt, thank you for believing in Boss Beauties since the beginning of our journey. We're honored to have you all involved in what we're building through BB.

And to the Collective Book Studio and Simon & Schuster teams, thank you for helping us make this book a reality! We could not have brought this book to life without your industry expertise, your vision, and your publishing knowledge.

Illustrations by Marion Ben-Lisa.
Cover and Interior Design by Rachel Lopez Metzger.

Library of Congress Cataloging-in-Publication Data available.
ISBN: 978-1-68555-348-7
Ebook ISBN: 978-1-68555-568-9
Library of Congress Control Number: 2023906129

Printed using Forest Stewardship Council certified stock from sustainably managed forests.

Manufactured in China.
10 9 8 7 6 5 4 3 2 1

The Collective Book Studio®
Oakland, California
www.thecollectivebook.studio